Air Fryer Hamburgers

Delicious and Healthy Burger Recipes Perfectly Cooked in Your Air Fryer

AIR FRYER HAMBURGERS

First edition. January 17, 2024.

Copyright © 2024 john ahmad.

ISBN: 979-8224077281

Written by john ahmad.

Table of Contents

John Ahmad

Chapter 1: Introduction to Air Fryer Cooking

Why Air Fryers Are Great for Burgers

Air fryers have taken the culinary world by storm with their ability to create crispy, delicious dishes using significantly less oil than traditional frying methods. When it comes to burgers, air fryers offer a fantastic alternative to pan-frying or grilling. In this chapter, we'll explore why air fryers are the perfect kitchen tool for cooking hamburgers to perfection.

Benefits of Air Frying Burgers

Healthier Cooking: Air frying allows you to enjoy the taste and texture of fried foods without the excessive oil. By using hot air circulation, air fryers crisp up the exterior of burgers while keeping the inside juicy.

Reduced Fat Content: Traditional deep frying can result in burgers soaked in oil. With an air fryer, excess fat drips away during cooking, leading to a leaner, healthier meal.

Speed and Convenience: Air fryers preheat quickly and cook burgers evenly in a fraction of the time it takes to grill or pan-fry them. This makes them ideal for busy weeknight dinners.

Less Mess: Say goodbye to splattering oil and a greasy stovetop. Air fryers are designed to contain messes and are easy to clean.

Versatile Cooking: Beyond burgers, air fryers can be used for a wide range of dishes, from chicken wings to vegetables, making them a versatile addition to your kitchen.

Essential Tips for Air Frying

Before you dive into cooking burgers in your air fryer, here are some essential tips to ensure success:

Preheat Your Air Fryer: Just like an oven, it's important to preheat your air fryer. This helps in achieving a crispy exterior on your burgers.

Use the Right Temperature: Most burger recipes call for a temperature of around 375°F (190°C). This ensures that the burgers cook through while developing a golden-brown crust.

Don't Overcrowd the Basket: To allow proper air circulation, avoid overcrowding the air fryer basket. Cook burgers in batches if necessary.

Oil or Non-Stick Spray: While air fryers use less oil, a light coating of cooking spray or a brush of oil on the burger patties can enhance their texture and flavor.

Flip When Needed: Flip the burgers halfway through cooking for even browning. This step is crucial for achieving that perfect crust.

Check for Doneness: Use a meat thermometer to ensure that your burgers reach a safe internal temperature of 160°F (71°C) for ground beef.

Resting Time: Allow your burgers to rest for a few minutes after cooking. This allows the juices to redistribute, keeping the meat moist.

Experiment and Have Fun: Don't be afraid to get creative with burger toppings and seasonings. Air fryers offer a wide range of possibilities for flavor experimentation.

As we progress through this cookbook, you'll discover a variety of burger recipes tailored to the unique advantages of air frying. Whether you're a seasoned air fryer chef or just getting started, you'll find these recipes easy to follow and the results incredibly satisfying.

Now that you understand why air fryers are fantastic for cooking burgers let's dive into crafting the perfect patty in Chapter 2!

Chapter 2: Choosing the Perfect Burger Patty

In the world of burger crafting, selecting the right meat and flavorings is crucial to achieving a delicious and satisfying burger experience. In this chapter, we'll delve into the art of choosing the perfect burger patty for your air fryer creations.

Ground Meat Selection

The type of meat you choose forms the foundation of your burger, and each option brings its own unique flavors and characteristics. Let's explore some common ground meat selections for your air fryer hamburgers:

1. Ground Beef

80/20 Ground Beef: This classic choice contains 80% lean meat and 20% fat. The fat content adds richness and juiciness to your burgers. It's perfect for classic, indulgent burgers.

90/10 Ground Beef: For a leaner option, opt for 90% lean meat and 10% fat. While it's healthier, it may result in slightly drier burgers, so be mindful not to overcook them.

Ground Chuck: Ground chuck comes from the shoulder of the cow and has a higher fat content, around 15-20%. It's often considered ideal for burgers because it combines flavor and juiciness.

Blended Beef: Some burger enthusiasts blend different cuts of beef, like chuck, sirloin, and brisket, to create a custom blend. This allows you to balance flavor and fat to your liking.

2. Ground Chicken

Ground chicken is a lean and healthy option for burger patties. It has a milder flavor than beef, making it a versatile canvas for a variety of seasonings and toppings. Be cautious not to overcook chicken patties, as they can dry out quickly.

3. Ground Turkey

Ground turkey is another lean alternative to beef. It's lower in fat but can still yield juicy burgers if seasoned and cooked properly. Consider using a mix of light and dark meat for added flavor.

5. Veggie and Plant-Based Options

If you're vegetarian or looking for a meatless option, there are various plant-based burger patties available in stores or you can make your own using ingredients like mushrooms, beans, or tofu. These can be air-fried just like traditional meat patties.

Seasoning and Flavoring Options

Once you've selected your ground meat, it's time to infuse your burger patties with flavor. Here are some seasoning and flavoring options to consider:

1. Classic Seasonings

Salt and Pepper: A simple combination that enhances the natural flavors of the meat.

Garlic and Onion Powder: Adds depth and aroma to your patties.

Paprika: Provides a subtle smoky flavor and a vibrant color.

Worcestershire Sauce: Adds umami richness and depth to the meat.

2. Herbs and Spices

Rosemary: Fresh or dried rosemary lends an earthy, aromatic note.

Thyme: Fresh thyme leaves or ground thyme can elevate your burger's flavor.

Cumin: Adds warmth and a touch of smokiness.

Chili Powder: For those who crave a bit of heat.

3. Condiments and Sauces

BBQ Sauce: Mix it directly into the meat for a BBQ-infused burger.

Soy Sauce: A splash of soy sauce can provide an umami kick.

Mustard: Adds tanginess and a hint of spice.

4. Cheese and Stuffing

Cheese-Stuffed Patties: Experiment by placing cheese (like cheddar, blue cheese, or feta) in the center of your patty for a gooey surprise when you bite in.

Bacon Bits: Mix bits of cooked bacon into the meat for a smoky, savory twist.

5. Custom Blends

Get creative and mix and match your seasonings and flavorings to create a signature burger that suits your taste preferences.

When crafting your perfect burger patty, don't be afraid to experiment with different combinations of meat and flavors. Your air fryer is a versatile tool that can handle a wide range of burger variations.

In the next chapters, we'll dive into specific recipes that put these patty choices and flavor options to delicious use.

Now that you've mastered the art of patty selection and seasoning, let's move on to Chapter 3, where we'll explore the classic beef burger in all its glory!

Chapter 3: Classic Beef Burgers

Beef burgers are the quintessential American comfort food, and they're the perfect canvas for exploring the wonders of air fryer cooking. In this chapter, we'll delve into the world of classic beef burgers, starting with a traditional recipe and then exploring some mouthwatering cheeseburger variations.

Traditional Beef Burger Recipe
Ingredients:

- 1 pound (450g) ground beef (80/20 blend for juiciness)
- 1/2 teaspoon salt
- 1/4 teaspoon black pepper
- 1/4 teaspoon garlic powder
- 4 hamburger buns
- Your choice of toppings (lettuce, tomato, onion, pickles, etc.)
- Condiments (ketchup, mustard, mayonnaise, etc.)

Instructions:

1. Preheat Your Air Fryer: Preheat your air fryer to 375°F (190°C) for about 5 minutes.

Prepare the Burger Patties:

1. In a mixing bowl, combine the ground beef, salt, black pepper, and garlic powder.
2. Gently mix the ingredients until well combined. Be careful not to overwork the meat, as it can make the burgers tough.
3. Divide the mixture into 4 equal portions and shape them into patties, slightly larger than the size of your buns to account for shrinkage during cooking.

Air Fry the Patties:

1. Place the burger patties in a single layer in the air fryer basket, ensuring there's some space between them.
2. Cook for approximately 10-12 minutes, flipping the patties halfway through. Cooking times may vary depending on your air fryer, so use a meat thermometer to ensure the patties reach an internal temperature of 160°F (71°C).

Assemble Your Burgers:

1. While the patties are cooking, you can lightly toast the burger buns in the air fryer for about 1-2 minutes.
2. Once the patties are cooked, remove them from the air fryer and let them rest for a few minutes.
3. Assemble your burgers with your favorite toppings and condiments. Consider adding cheese while the patties are still hot for a melty, gooey finish.

Serve and Enjoy:

1. Serve your classic beef burgers immediately. Enjoy the juicy,

flavorful goodness!

Cheeseburger Variations

1. Classic Cheeseburger:

Follow the traditional beef burger recipe but add a slice of your favorite cheese (American, cheddar, Swiss, etc.) to each patty during the last minute of air frying. The cheese will melt and create a creamy, gooey layer over the burger.

2. Bacon and Cheeseburger:

Add cooked bacon strips to your classic cheeseburger for a smoky, savory twist. Stack the bacon on top of the cheese for a burst of flavor with every bite.

3. Mushroom Swiss Burger:

Sautéed mushrooms and Swiss cheese pair beautifully with beef. Sauté sliced mushrooms in a bit of butter and garlic until they're tender, then top your burger with the mushrooms and a slice of Swiss cheese.

4. Blue Cheese Burger:

For a bold flavor profile, crumble blue cheese on top of your burger patties during the last minute of cooking. The creamy and tangy blue cheese complements the richness of the beef.

5. Patty Melt:

Create a patty melt by sandwiching your beef patty, sautéed onions, and Swiss cheese between slices of rye bread. Air fry the assembled sandwich until the cheese melts and the bread becomes crispy.

Classic beef burgers are a timeless favorite, and with the magic of your air fryer, you can have them ready in no time. Experiment with these variations or create your own cheeseburger masterpiece. In the next chapters, we'll explore more burger options, including chicken, turkey, and even seafood!

Chapter 4: Creative Chicken Burgers

Chicken burgers are a delightful alternative to beef, offering a lighter and leaner option while still delivering loads of flavor. In this chapter, we'll explore two creative chicken burger recipes: the Spicy Buffalo Chicken Burger and the Teriyaki Pineapple Chicken Burger.

Spicy Buffalo Chicken Burger

Ingredients:

- 1 pound (450g) ground chicken
- 1/4 cup breadcrumbs
- 1/4 cup hot sauce (adjust to taste)
- 1/4 cup finely chopped celery
- 1/4 cup crumbled blue cheese
- 1/2 teaspoon garlic powder
- Salt and pepper to taste
- 4 hamburger buns
- Lettuce leaves
- Ranch or blue cheese dressing
- Sliced tomatoes (optional)

Instructions:

1. Preheat Your Air Fryer: Preheat your air fryer to 375°F (190°C) for about 5 minutes.

Prepare the Chicken Patties:

1. In a mixing bowl, combine the ground chicken, breadcrumbs, hot sauce, chopped celery, crumbled blue cheese, garlic powder, salt, and pepper.
2. Mix until all the ingredients are evenly distributed.
3. Divide the mixture into 4 equal portions and shape them into

patties

.

Air Fry the Chicken Patties:

1. Place the chicken patties in a single layer in the air fryer basket.
2. Cook for approximately 10-12 minutes, flipping the patties halfway through. Ensure the patties reach an internal temperature of 165°F (74°C).

Assemble Your Buffalo Chicken Burgers:

1. While the patties are cooking, you can toast the burger buns in the air fryer for about 1-2 minutes.
2. Once the chicken patties are cooked and slightly crispy, assemble your burgers with lettuce leaves, a drizzle of ranch or blue cheese dressing, and optional tomato slices.
3. Serve your Spicy Buffalo Chicken Burgers with extra hot sauce for those who crave more heat.

Teriyaki Pineapple Chicken Burger
Ingredients:

- 1 pound (450g) ground chicken
- 1/4 cup teriyaki sauce
- 1/4 cup crushed pineapple, drained
- 1/4 cup finely chopped red bell pepper
- 1/4 cup sliced green onions
- 1/2 teaspoon garlic powder
- Salt and pepper to taste
- 4 hamburger buns
- Lettuce leaves
- Sliced pineapple rings
- Teriyaki glaze (store-bought or homemade)

Instructions:

Preheat Your Air Fryer: Preheat your air fryer to 375°F (190°C) for about 5 minutes.

Prepare the Chicken Patties:

In a mixing bowl, combine the ground chicken, teriyaki sauce, crushed pineapple, chopped red bell pepper, sliced green onions, garlic powder, salt, and pepper.

Mix until all the ingredients are well incorporated.

Divide the mixture into 4 equal portions and shape them into patties.

Air Fry the Chicken Patties:

Place the chicken patties in a single layer in the air fryer basket.

Cook for approximately 10-12 minutes, flipping the patties halfway through. Ensure the patties reach an internal temperature of 165°F (74°C).

Assemble Your Teriyaki Pineapple Chicken Burgers:

While the patties are cooking, you can toast the burger buns in the air fryer for about 1-2 minutes.

Once the chicken patties are cooked and slightly caramelized, assemble your burgers with lettuce leaves, a sliced pineapple ring, and a drizzle of teriyaki glaze.

Serve your Teriyaki Pineapple Chicken Burgers with extra teriyaki sauce on the side for dipping.

These creative chicken burgers are bursting with flavor and are a delightful departure from the traditional beef patty. Whether you're craving a spicy kick or a sweet and savory twist, these recipes have you covered.

Chapter 5: Mouthwatering Turkey Burgers

Turkey burgers offer a lean and flavorful alternative to beef, and when cooked in the air fryer, they become juicy and delicious. In this chapter, we'll explore two mouthwatering turkey burger recipes: the Juicy Turkey and Avocado Burger and the Cranberry and Brie Turkey Burger.

Juicy Turkey and Avocado Burger

Ingredients:

- 1 pound (450g) ground turkey
- 1 ripe avocado, mashed
- 1/4 cup breadcrumbs
- 1/4 cup finely chopped red onion
- 1/4 cup chopped fresh cilantro
- 1/2 teaspoon garlic powder
- Salt and pepper to taste
- 4 hamburger buns
- Lettuce leaves
- Sliced tomatoes
- Sliced red onion
- Sliced avocado (optional)

Instructions:

Preheat Your Air Fryer: Preheat your air fryer to 375°F (190°C) for about 5 minutes.

Prepare the Turkey Patties:

In a mixing bowl, combine the ground turkey, mashed avocado, breadcrumbs, chopped red onion, chopped cilantro, garlic powder, salt, and pepper.

Mix until all the ingredients are well combined.

Divide the mixture into 4 equal portions and shape them into patties.

Air Fry the Turkey Patties:

Place the turkey patties in a single layer in the air fryer basket.

Cook for approximately 10-12 minutes, flipping the patties halfway through. Ensure the patties reach an internal temperature of 165°F (74°C).

Assemble Your Juicy Turkey and Avocado Burgers:

While the patties are cooking, you can toast the burger buns in the air fryer for about 1-2 minutes.

Once the turkey patties are cooked and slightly golden, assemble your burgers with lettuce leaves, sliced tomatoes, sliced red onion, and optional avocado slices.

Serve your Juicy Turkey and Avocado Burgers with your favorite condiments.

Cranberry and Brie Turkey Burger
Ingredients:

- 1 pound (450g) ground turkey
- 1/4 cup dried cranberries, finely chopped
- 1/4 cup Brie cheese, diced
- 1/4 cup finely chopped red onion
- 1/4 teaspoon dried thyme
- Salt and pepper to taste
- 4 hamburger buns
- Baby spinach leaves
- Cranberry sauce
- Sliced Brie cheese (optional)

Instructions:

Preheat Your Air Fryer: Preheat your air fryer to 375°F (190°C) for about 5 minutes.

Prepare the Turkey Patties:

In a mixing bowl, combine the ground turkey, chopped dried cranberries, diced Brie cheese, chopped red onion, dried thyme, salt, and pepper.

Mix until all the ingredients are evenly incorporated.

Divide the mixture into 4 equal portions and shape them into patties.

Air Fry the Turkey Patties:

Place the turkey patties in a single layer in the air fryer basket.

Cook for approximately 10-12 minutes, flipping the patties halfway through. Ensure the patties reach an internal temperature of 165°F (74°C).

Assemble Your Cranberry and Brie Turkey Burgers:

While the patties are cooking, you can toast the burger buns in the air fryer for about 1-2 minutes.

Once the turkey patties are cooked and slightly caramelized, assemble your burgers with baby spinach leaves, a drizzle of cranberry sauce, and optional sliced Brie cheese.

Serve your Cranberry and Brie Turkey Burgers with a side of extra cranberry sauce for dipping.

These turkey burger recipes are bursting with unique flavors and are perfect for those seeking a lighter burger option. Whether you prefer the creamy goodness of avocado or the sweet and savory combination of cranberry and Brie, these burgers are sure to satisfy your taste buds.

Chapter 6: Sensational Seafood Burgers

Seafood burgers offer a fresh and light alternative to traditional meat patties. In this chapter, we'll explore two sensational seafood burger recipes: the Salmon and Dill Burger and the Shrimp and Mango Burger.

Salmon and Dill Burger

Ingredients:

- 1 pound (450g) fresh salmon fillets, skin removed
- 1/4 cup breadcrumbs
- 1/4 cup finely chopped fresh dill
- Zest of 1 lemon
- 1/4 teaspoon garlic powder
- Salt and pepper to taste
- 4 hamburger buns
- Mixed greens or arugula
- Sliced cucumber
- Lemon wedges
- Dill sauce (yogurt-based sauce with fresh dill)

Instructions:

Preheat Your Air Fryer: Preheat your air fryer to 375°F (190°C) for about 5 minutes.

Prepare the Salmon Patties:

Cut the salmon fillets into small pieces and place them in a food processor.

Pulse the salmon until it's finely chopped but not pureed.

Transfer the chopped salmon to a mixing bowl and add breadcrumbs, chopped dill, lemon zest, garlic powder, salt, and pepper.

Mix until all the ingredients are well combined.

Divide the mixture into 4 equal portions and shape them into patties

Air Fry the Salmon Patties:

Place the salmon patties in a single layer in the air fryer basket.

Cook for approximately 10-12 minutes, flipping the patties halfway through. Ensure the patties reach an internal temperature of 145°F (63°C).

Assemble Your Salmon and Dill Burgers:

While the patties are cooking, you can toast the burger buns in the air fryer for about 1-2 minutes.

Once the salmon patties are cooked and slightly crispy, assemble your burgers with mixed greens, sliced cucumber, and a drizzle of dill sauce.

Serve your Salmon and Dill Burgers with lemon wedges for an extra burst of freshness.

Shrimp and Mango Burger

Ingredients:

- 1/2 pound (225g) large shrimp, peeled and deveined
- 1/2 cup diced ripe mango
- 1/4 cup breadcrumbs
- 1/4 cup finely chopped red bell pepper
- 1/4 cup finely chopped red onion
- 1/2 teaspoon ground cumin
- Salt and pepper to taste
- 4 hamburger buns
- Baby spinach leaves
- Sliced avocado
- Sriracha mayo (mix sriracha sauce with mayonnaise)

Instructions:

Preheat Your Air Fryer: Preheat your air fryer to 375°F (190°C) for about 5 minutes.

Prepare the Shrimp Patties:

Place the peeled and deveined shrimp in a food processor.

Pulse the shrimp until it's finely chopped but not pureed.

Transfer the chopped shrimp to a mixing bowl and add diced mango, breadcrumbs, chopped red bell pepper, chopped red onion, ground cumin, salt, and pepper.

Mix until all the ingredients are well combined.

Divide the mixture into 4 equal portions and shape them into patties.

Air Fry the Shrimp Patties:

Place the shrimp patties in a single layer in the air fryer basket.

Cook for approximately 8-10 minutes, flipping the patties halfway through. Ensure the patties reach an internal temperature of 145°F (63°C).

Assemble Your Shrimp and Mango Burgers:

While the patties are cooking, you can toast the burger buns in the air fryer for about 1-2 minutes.

Once the shrimp patties are cooked and slightly golden, assemble your burgers with baby spinach leaves, sliced avocado, and a drizzle of sriracha mayo.

Serve your Shrimp and Mango Burgers with a side of extra sriracha mayo for dipping.

These seafood burger recipes showcase the fresh flavors of salmon and shrimp, making for a delightful and lighter burger experience. Whether you're a seafood lover or simply looking to explore new burger horizons, these recipes are sure to please.

Chapter 7: Veggie and Plant-Based Burgers

Veggie and plant-based burgers have gained popularity for their health benefits and eco-friendliness. In this chapter, we'll explore two delicious options: Homemade Veggie Burger Patties and a Portobello Mushroom Burger.

Homemade Veggie Burger Patties

Ingredients:

- 1 can (15 ounces) black beans, drained and rinsed
- 1/2 cup cooked quinoa
- 1/2 cup rolled oats
- 1/4 cup finely chopped onion
- 1/4 cup finely chopped bell pepper (any color)
- 1/4 cup grated carrot
- 2 cloves garlic, minced
- 1 teaspoon chili powder
- 1/2 teaspoon cumin
- Salt and pepper to taste
- Cooking spray or oil for air frying
- 4 whole-grain burger buns
- Lettuce leaves
- Sliced tomatoes
- Sliced red onion
- Your favorite condiments

Instructions:

Preheat Your Air Fryer: Preheat your air fryer to 375°F (190°C) for about 5 minutes.

Prepare the Veggie Burger Patties:

In a food processor, combine the black beans, cooked quinoa, rolled oats, chopped onion, chopped bell pepper, grated carrot, minced garlic, chili powder, cumin, salt, and pepper.

Pulse until the mixture comes together but is still slightly chunky. You don't want it to be pureed.

Divide the mixture into 4 equal portions and shape them into patties.

Air Fry the Veggie Burger Patties:

Lightly grease the air fryer basket with cooking spray or oil.

Place the veggie burger patties in a single layer in the air fryer basket.

Cook for approximately 10-12 minutes, flipping the patties halfway through. They should be golden and slightly crispy on the outside.

Assemble Your Homemade Veggie Burgers:

While the patties are cooking, you can toast the whole-grain burger buns in the air fryer for about 1-2 minutes.

Once the veggie burger patties are cooked and slightly crispy, assemble your burgers with lettuce leaves, sliced tomatoes, sliced red onion, and your favorite condiments.

Serve your Homemade Veggie Burgers with a side of sweet potato fries or a crisp salad.

Portobello Mushroom Burger
Ingredients:

- 4 large Portobello mushroom caps, stems removed
- 2 tablespoons balsamic vinegar
- 2 tablespoons olive oil
- 2 cloves garlic, minced
- 1 teaspoon dried thyme
- Salt and pepper to taste
- 4 whole-grain burger buns
- Baby spinach leaves
- Roasted red bell peppers (store-bought or homemade)
- Sliced red onion
- Vegan or regular mayo

Instructions:

Preheat Your Air Fryer: Preheat your air fryer to 375°F (190°C) for about 5 minutes.

Prepare the Portobello Mushrooms:

In a bowl, whisk together the balsamic vinegar, olive oil, minced garlic, dried thyme, salt, and pepper.

Brush this marinade over the Portobello mushroom caps, ensuring they're well coated.

Air Fry the Portobello Mushroom Caps:

Place the marinated Portobello mushroom caps in the air fryer basket, gill side up.

Cook for approximately 10-12 minutes, flipping the caps halfway through. They should be tender and slightly caramelized.

Assemble Your Portobello Mushroom Burgers:

While the mushrooms are cooking, you can toast the whole-grain burger buns in the air fryer for about 1-2 minutes.

Once the Portobello mushroom caps are cooked, assemble your burgers with baby spinach leaves, roasted red bell peppers, sliced red onion, and vegan or regular mayo.

Serve your Portobello Mushroom Burgers with a side of mixed greens or coleslaw.

These veggie and plant-based burger options are not only delicious but also offer a nutritious and cruelty-free alternative to traditional meat patties. Whether you opt for homemade veggie burger patties or the earthy flavors of a Portobello mushroom cap, these recipes are sure to satisfy your taste buds.

Chapter 8: Low-Carb and Keto Burgers

If you're following a low-carb or keto lifestyle, you can still enjoy delicious burgers without the guilt. In this chapter, we'll explore two low-carb and keto-friendly burger options: Lettuce Wrap Burgers and Almond Flour Buns.

Lettuce Wrap Burgers

Ingredients:

- 1 pound (450g) ground beef (80/20 blend for juiciness)
- Salt and pepper to taste
- 4 large iceberg lettuce leaves (or butter lettuce leaves)
- Your choice of toppings (cheese, bacon, avocado, onions, etc.)
- Sugar-free ketchup or mayo (optional)

Instructions:

Preheat Your Air Fryer: Preheat your air fryer to 375°F (190°C) for about 5 minutes.

Prepare the Burger Patties:

In a mixing bowl, season the ground beef with salt and pepper.

Divide the mixture into 4 equal portions and shape them into thin patties, slightly larger than the size of your lettuce leaves.

Air Fry the Burger Patties:

Place the burger patties in a single layer in the air fryer basket.

Cook for approximately 8-10 minutes, flipping the patties halfway through. Cooking times may vary depending on your air fryer, so use a meat thermometer to ensure the patties reach an internal temperature of 160°F (71°C).

Assemble Your Lettuce Wrap Burgers:

While the patties are cooking, carefully separate 4 large lettuce leaves, which will serve as your burger "buns."

Once the burger patties are cooked, place each patty on a lettuce leaf.

Add your choice of low-carb toppings and condiments, such as cheese, bacon, avocado, onions, or sugar-free ketchup or mayo.

Fold the lettuce leaf around the burger and toppings, securing it with a toothpick if needed.

Serve and Enjoy:

Serve your Lettuce Wrap Burgers immediately. They offer all the flavors of a traditional burger without the carb-heavy bun.

Almond Flour Buns

Ingredients:

- 2 cups almond flour
- 1/4 cup psyllium husk powder
- 1 teaspoon baking powder
- 1/2 teaspoon salt
- 2 large eggs
- 1/4 cup olive oil
- 1/4 cup warm water

Instructions:

Preheat Your Air Fryer: Preheat your air fryer to 375°F (190°C) for about 5 minutes.

Prepare the Almond Flour Buns:

In a mixing bowl, combine the almond flour, psyllium husk powder, baking powder, and salt.

In a separate bowl, whisk together the eggs, olive oil, and warm water.

Combine Wet and Dry Ingredients:

Pour the wet ingredients into the dry ingredients and stir until a dough forms.

Divide the dough into 4 equal portions and shape them into burger bun-sized rounds.

Air Fry the Almond Flour Buns:

Place the almond flour buns in the air fryer basket, ensuring there's some space between them.

Cook for approximately 10-12 minutes until the buns are firm and slightly golden.

Assemble Your Burgers:

Once the almond flour buns are cooked and slightly cooled, use them as the "buns" for your low-carb and keto-friendly burgers.

Assemble your burgers with your choice of toppings and condiments.

These low-carb and keto burger options allow you to enjoy the deliciousness of burgers while staying within your dietary preferences. Whether you opt for the refreshing crunch of lettuce wraps or the satisfying texture of almond flour buns, these recipes cater to your health-conscious needs.

Chapter 9: Unique Burger Toppings and Homemade Burger Sauces

Elevate your burger game with unique toppings and homemade sauces that add flavor and excitement to every bite. In this chapter, we'll explore Gourmet Burger Toppings and Homemade Burger Sauces that will take your burger creations to the next level.

Gourmet Burger Toppings

Caramelized Onions:

Ingredients:

- 2 large onions, thinly sliced
- 2 tablespoons butter
- 1 tablespoon olive oil
- 1 teaspoon sugar (optional)
- Salt and pepper to taste

Instructions:

1. In a skillet, heat the butter and olive oil over medium-low heat.
2. Add the thinly sliced onions and cook slowly, stirring occasionally, until they become soft and golden brown, about 30-40 minutes.
3. If desired, sprinkle with sugar to aid in caramelization.
4. Season with salt and pepper.

Balsamic Glazed Mushrooms:

Ingredients:

- 8 ounces (225g) mushrooms, sliced
- 2 tablespoons balsamic vinegar

- 1 tablespoon olive oil
- 1 clove garlic, minced
- Salt and pepper to taste

Instructions:

1. In a skillet, heat the olive oil over medium heat.
2. Add the sliced mushrooms and cook until they start to brown, about 5 minutes.
3. Add minced garlic and cook for another minute.
4. Stir in balsamic vinegar and continue cooking until the mushrooms are coated and the liquid reduces.

Guacamole:
Ingredients:

- 2 ripe avocados, mashed
- 1/4 cup diced red onion
- 1/4 cup diced tomato
- 2 tablespoons chopped cilantro
- 1 clove garlic, minced
- Juice of 1 lime
- Salt and pepper to taste

Instructions:

1. In a bowl, combine mashed avocados, diced red onion, diced tomato, chopped cilantro, minced garlic, lime juice, salt, and pepper.
2. Mix until all ingredients are well incorporated.

Homemade Burger Sauces
Classic Burger Sauce:
Ingredients:

- 1/2 cup mayonnaise
- 2 tablespoons ketchup
- 1 tablespoon yellow mustard
- 1 tablespoon sweet pickle relish
- 1 teaspoon white vinegar
- 1/2 teaspoon sugar
- 1/4 teaspoon garlic powder
- 1/4 teaspoon onion powder
- Salt and pepper to taste

Instructions:

1. In a bowl, whisk together all the ingredients until well blended.
2. Taste and adjust the seasonings as needed.

Sriracha Aioli:
Ingredients:

- 1/2 cup mayonnaise
- 1-2 tablespoons sriracha sauce (adjust to taste)
- 1 clove garlic, minced
- Juice of 1/2 lemon
- Salt and pepper to taste

Instructions:

1. In a bowl, combine mayonnaise, sriracha sauce, minced garlic, lemon juice, salt, and pepper.
2. Adjust the sriracha sauce to your preferred level of heat.

Honey Mustard Sauce:
Ingredients:

- 1/4 cup mayonnaise
- 2 tablespoons Dijon mustard
- 2 tablespoons honey
- 1 tablespoon lemon juice
- Salt and pepper to taste

Instructions:

In a bowl, whisk together mayonnaise, Dijon mustard, honey, lemon juice, salt, and pepper.

Taste and adjust the honey and mustard to achieve the desired balance of sweetness and tanginess.

These gourmet burger toppings and homemade burger sauces are designed to tantalize your taste buds and add a gourmet touch to your burger creations. Mix and match toppings and sauces to create your own unique burger masterpieces.

Chapter 10: Perfectly Pairing Sides

A burger meal isn't complete without some delicious sides to accompany it. In this chapter, we'll explore two fantastic side options that perfectly complement your burger experience: Crispy Air Fryer Fries and Coleslaw and Salad Ideas.

Crispy Air Fryer Fries

Ingredients:

- 4 large russet potatoes, peeled and cut into fries
- 2 tablespoons olive oil
- 1 teaspoon paprika
- 1/2 teaspoon garlic powder
- Salt and pepper to taste
- Cooking spray or oil for air frying

Instructions:

Preheat Your Air Fryer: Preheat your air fryer to 375°F (190°C) for about 5 minutes.

Prepare the Fries:

In a large bowl, toss the cut potato fries with olive oil, paprika, garlic powder, salt, and pepper until they are well coated.

Air Fry the Fries:

Lightly grease the air fryer basket with cooking spray or oil.

Arrange the seasoned fries in a single layer in the air fryer basket, ensuring they are not crowded.

Cook for approximately 20-25 minutes, shaking the basket or flipping the fries halfway through, until they are golden brown and crispy.

Serve and Enjoy:

Sprinkle with additional salt if desired and serve your Crispy Air Fryer Fries alongside your burgers. These fries are a healthier alternative to traditional deep-fried fries, yet they're just as satisfying.

Coleslaw and Salad Ideas
Classic Coleslaw:
Ingredients:

- 4 cups shredded cabbage (green and purple)
- 1/2 cup shredded carrots
- 1/4 cup chopped fresh parsley
- 1/2 cup mayonnaise
- 2 tablespoons apple cider vinegar
- 1 tablespoon honey
- Salt and pepper to taste

Instructions:

1. In a large bowl, combine shredded cabbage, shredded carrots, and chopped parsley.
2. In a separate bowl, whisk together mayonnaise, apple cider vinegar, honey, salt, and pepper.
3. Pour the dressing over the cabbage mixture and toss until everything is well coated.
4. Refrigerate for at least 30 minutes before serving to allow the flavors to meld.

Garden Salad:
Ingredients:

- Mixed greens or your choice of lettuce
- Sliced cucumber
- Cherry tomatoes, halved
- Sliced red onion
- Kalamata olives (optional)
- Feta cheese (optional)
- Balsamic vinaigrette or your favorite salad dressing

Instructions:

1. In a large bowl, combine mixed greens, sliced cucumber, cherry tomatoes, sliced red onion, and any optional ingredients you desire.
2. Toss with your preferred salad dressing just before serving.

This fresh Garden Salad is a light and refreshing side that complements the richness of your burger.

These side dishes offer a range of flavors and textures to enhance your burger experience. Whether you're a fan of crispy fries, creamy coleslaw, or a refreshing salad, these sides are the perfect accompaniments to your burger creations.

Chapter 11: Burger Bites and Sliders

Sometimes, smaller bites are just what you need to satisfy your burger cravings. In this chapter, we'll explore Burger Bites and Sliders—perfect for parties, snacking, or when you want to enjoy a variety of burger flavors without committing to a full-sized burger.

Mini Burger Party Platters

Ingredients:

- Mini burger buns or slider rolls
- Assorted burger patties (beef, chicken, turkey, or veggie)
- Gourmet toppings (caramelized onions, balsamic glazed mushrooms, guacamole)
- Homemade burger sauces (classic, sriracha aioli, honey mustard)
- Lettuce leaves, sliced tomatoes, and other fresh veggies
- Sliced cheeses (cheddar, Swiss, Brie)
- Toothpicks or small skewers for securing mini burgers

Instructions:

Prepare Mini Burger Patties:

Depending on your preference, prepare mini-sized versions of your favorite burger patties using ground meat or veggie burger mixtures.

Cook the mini patties in your air fryer or on a stovetop griddle until they reach the desired level of doneness.

Assemble Mini Burgers:

Slice the mini burger buns or slider rolls in half.

Assemble your mini burgers with a variety of toppings, sauces, fresh veggies, and cheese.

Secure each mini burger with a toothpick or small skewer.

Create a Platter:

Arrange the mini burgers on a platter, making sure to include a variety of flavors and toppings.

Add some lettuce leaves, sliced tomatoes, or pickles on the side for freshness.

Serve and Enjoy:

Your Mini Burger Party Platter is ready to be enjoyed by your guests. They can mix and match to create their perfect bite-sized burger.

Slider Sauce Sampler
Ingredients:

- Classic Burger Sauce
- Sriracha Aioli
- Honey Mustard Sauce
- Ketchup and mustard
- BBQ sauce
- Hot sauce
- Ranch dressing

Instructions:

Prepare Sauces:

Prepare each sauce separately and transfer them to small serving bowls or ramekins.

For variety, consider mixing ketchup and mustard for a classic burger sauce, or adding hot sauce to ranch dressing for a spicy twist.

Arrange the Sampler:

Place the sauce bowls on a serving platter or tray.

Label each sauce to make it easy for your guests to identify their favorites.

Serve and Enjoy:

Your Slider Sauce Sampler is ready to accompany your Mini Burger Party Platter.

Encourage your guests to dip, drizzle, and savor the various sauces with their mini burgers.

These burger bites and sliders are perfect for parties, gatherings, or when you simply want to enjoy a variety of flavors in smaller portions. With an assortment of toppings and sauces, you can customize each mini burger to your heart's content.

Chapter 12: International Burger Flavors

Travel the culinary world without leaving your kitchen by exploring international burger flavors. In this chapter, we'll take your taste buds on a journey with two flavorful options: the Greek Gyro Burger and the Thai-inspired Burger.

Greek Gyro Burger

Ingredients:

For the Gyro Burger Patties:

- 1 pound (450g) ground lamb or beef (or a mixture of both)
- 2 cloves garlic, minced
- 1 small onion, grated
- 1 teaspoon dried oregano
- 1/2 teaspoon ground cumin
- Salt and pepper to taste

For the Tzatziki Sauce:

- 1 cup Greek yogurt
- 1/2 cucumber, grated and drained
- 2 cloves garlic, minced
- 1 tablespoon fresh lemon juice
- 1 tablespoon fresh dill, chopped
- Salt and pepper to taste

For Assembly:

- Pita bread or burger buns
- Sliced tomatoes
- Sliced red onion
- Fresh lettuce leaves

Instructions:

Prepare the Gyro Burger Patties:

In a bowl, combine the ground lamb or beef with minced garlic, grated onion, dried oregano, ground cumin, salt, and pepper.

Mix until all the ingredients are well combined.

Divide the mixture into 4 equal portions and shape them into patties.

Air Fry the Gyro Burger Patties:

Preheat your air fryer to 375°F (190°C) for about 5 minutes.

Place the gyro burger patties in a single layer in the air fryer basket.

Cook for approximately 10-12 minutes, flipping the patties halfway through. Ensure they reach your preferred level of doneness.

Prepare the Tzatziki Sauce:

In a bowl, combine Greek yogurt, grated and drained cucumber, minced garlic, fresh lemon juice, chopped dill, salt, and pepper.

Mix until the sauce is well blended.

Assemble Your Greek Gyro Burgers:

Warm the pita bread or burger buns in the air fryer for about 1-2 minutes.

Spread a generous dollop of tzatziki sauce on each piece of bread.

Place a gyro burger patty on top and add sliced tomatoes, red onion, and fresh lettuce leaves.

Serve your Greek Gyro Burgers with extra tzatziki sauce for dipping.

Thai-inspired Burger
Ingredients:
For the Burger Patties:

- 1 pound (450g) ground chicken
- 2 cloves garlic, minced
- 1 stalk lemongrass, finely chopped (tender part only)
- 1 small red chili pepper, finely chopped (adjust to taste)
- 2 tablespoons fresh cilantro, chopped
- 2 tablespoons fresh mint, chopped
- Zest of 1 lime
- Salt and pepper to taste

For the Peanut Sauce:

- 1/4 cup creamy peanut butter
- 2 tablespoons soy sauce
- 1 tablespoon fresh lime juice
- 1 tablespoon honey
- 1 teaspoon grated ginger
- 1 clove garlic, minced
- Water to thin (if needed)

For Assembly:

- Burger buns or lettuce wraps
- Sliced cucumber
- Fresh cilantro leaves
- Sliced red chili pepper (optional)

Instructions:

Prepare the Burger Patties:

In a bowl, combine ground chicken, minced garlic, finely chopped lemongrass, chopped red chili pepper, fresh cilantro, fresh mint, lime zest, salt, and pepper.

Mix until all the ingredients are well incorporated.

Divide the mixture into 4 equal portions and shape them into patties.

Air Fry the Burger Patties:

Preheat your air fryer to 375°F (190°C) for about 5 minutes.

Place the chicken burger patties in a single layer in the air fryer basket.

Cook for approximately 10-12 minutes, flipping the patties halfway through. Ensure they are cooked through.

Prepare the Peanut Sauce:

In a small saucepan, whisk together peanut butter, soy sauce, fresh lime juice, honey, grated ginger, and minced garlic.

Heat the mixture over low heat until it's smooth and slightly warmed. If the sauce is too thick, add a little water to thin it to your desired consistency.

Assemble Your Thai-inspired Burgers:

Warm the burger buns or prepare lettuce wraps.

Spread a spoonful of peanut sauce on each piece of bread or lettuce leaf.

Place a chicken burger patty on top and add sliced cucumber, fresh cilantro leaves, and sliced red chili pepper if you like a bit of heat.

Drizzle extra peanut sauce over the top.

These international-inspired burger flavors bring the vibrant and diverse tastes of Greece and Thailand to your plate. Whether you're craving the Mediterranean freshness of a gyro burger or the spicy, savory notes of a Thai-inspired burger, these recipes will transport you to distant lands through your taste buds.

Chapter 13: Burger Bowl Creations

If you're looking for a lighter way to enjoy the flavors of a burger, consider burger bowl creations. In this chapter, we'll explore two delicious options: the Burger Salad Bowl and the Deconstructed Burger Bowl.

Burger Salad Bowl
Ingredients:
For the Burger Patties:

- 1 pound (450g) ground beef
- Salt and pepper to taste
- Burger seasoning (optional)

For the Salad:

- Mixed greens or your choice of lettuce
- Sliced tomatoes
- Sliced red onion
- Sliced cucumber
- Sliced pickles
- Sliced cheese (cheddar, Swiss, or your favorite)
- Cooked and crumbled bacon (optional)
- Hard-boiled eggs, sliced (optional)

For the Dressing:

- 1/4 cup mayonnaise
- 1 tablespoon ketchup
- 1 tablespoon yellow mustard
- 1 tablespoon sweet pickle relish
- 1 teaspoon white vinegar
- 1/2 teaspoon sugar (optional)
- Salt and pepper to taste

Instructions:

Prepare the Burger Patties:

Season the ground beef with salt, pepper, and burger seasoning (if using).

Shape the seasoned beef into burger patties.

Air Fry the Burger Patties:

Preheat your air fryer to 375°F (190°C) for about 5 minutes.

Place the burger patties in a single layer in the air fryer basket.

Cook for approximately 10-12 minutes, flipping the patties halfway through. Ensure they reach your preferred level of doneness.

Prepare the Dressing:

In a small bowl, whisk together mayonnaise, ketchup, yellow mustard, sweet pickle relish, white vinegar, sugar (if using), salt, and pepper. Adjust the ingredients to your taste.

Assemble Your Burger Salad Bowl:

In a large bowl or individual serving bowls, start with a bed of mixed greens or your choice of lettuce.

Top the greens with sliced tomatoes, sliced red onion, sliced cucumber, sliced pickles, and your choice of cheese.

Place the cooked burger patties on top.

If desired, add cooked and crumbled bacon and sliced hard-boiled eggs.

Drizzle with Dressing:

Drizzle the dressing generously over the salad bowl.

Serve and Enjoy:

Your Burger Salad Bowl is ready to be enjoyed. Toss everything together for a satisfying burger-inspired salad experience.

Deconstructed Burger Bowl

Ingredients:

- Cooked and seasoned burger patties (beef, chicken, turkey, or veggie)
- Cooked bacon strips

- Sliced cheese (cheddar, Swiss, or your favorite)
- Sliced tomatoes
- Sliced red onion
- Sliced pickles
- Sliced avocado
- Cooked and crumbled ground beef (optional)
- Mixed greens or your choice of lettuce
- Burger seasoning (optional)

Instructions:

Prepare the Burger Patties:

Season and cook the burger patties of your choice to your preferred level of doneness.

If desired, you can also cook and crumble additional ground beef for extra flavor.

Assemble Your Deconstructed Burger Bowl:

In a large bowl or individual serving bowls, start with a bed of mixed greens or your choice of lettuce.

Arrange the cooked burger patties, bacon strips, sliced cheese, sliced tomatoes, sliced red onion, sliced pickles, sliced avocado, and cooked and crumbled ground beef (if using) around the lettuce.

Season and Serve:

If desired, sprinkle burger seasoning over the burger components for added flavor.

Serve and Enjoy:

Your Deconstructed Burger Bowl is ready to be enjoyed. Mix and match the components as you like for a customizable burger experience.

These burger bowl creations offer a unique twist on traditional burgers by presenting all the delicious components in a salad or deconstructed format. Whether you prefer the freshness of a salad or the ability to customize your bites, these recipes are perfect for those looking for a lighter burger option.

Chapter 14: Burger Fusion and Fusion Sauces

Experience the exciting world of burger fusion, where flavors from different cuisines come together to create mouthwatering combinations. In this chapter, we'll explore the Tex-Mex Burger Fusion and Fusion Burger Sauces to add a global twist to your burger repertoire.

Tex-Mex Burger Fusion

Ingredients:

For the Burger Patties:

- 1 pound (450g) ground beef
- 1 tablespoon taco seasoning
- Salt and pepper to taste
- For the Toppings:
- Sliced cheddar cheese
- Guacamole (store-bought or homemade)
- Sliced jalapeños
- Sliced red onion
- Sliced tomatoes
- Fresh cilantro leaves
- Burger buns or lettuce wraps

Instructions:

Prepare the Burger Patties:

Season the ground beef with taco seasoning, salt, and pepper.

Shape the seasoned beef into burger patties.

Air Fry the Burger Patties:

Preheat your air fryer to 375°F (190°C) for about 5 minutes.

Place the burger patties in a single layer in the air fryer basket.

Cook for approximately 10-12 minutes, flipping the patties halfway through. Ensure they reach your preferred level of doneness.

Assemble Your Tex-Mex Burger Fusion:

If using burger buns, lightly toast them in the air fryer for about 1-2 minutes.

Place a slice of cheddar cheese on each burger patty while they are still warm to allow it to melt.

Spread a generous dollop of guacamole on the bottom bun or lettuce wrap.

Top with the cheese-topped burger patty.

Add sliced jalapeños, red onion, tomatoes, and fresh cilantro leaves for a burst of Tex-Mex flavors.

Cover with the top bun or wrap in lettuce.

Serve and Enjoy:

Your Tex-Mex Burger Fusion is ready to be savored. Get ready for a flavor explosion with each bite!

Fusion Burger Sauces
Asian-inspired Sauce:
Ingredients:

- 1/4 cup soy sauce
- 2 tablespoons sesame oil
- 1 tablespoon honey
- 1 teaspoon grated ginger
- 1 clove garlic, minced
- 1/2 teaspoon sriracha sauce (adjust to taste)

Instructions:

In a bowl, whisk together soy sauce, sesame oil, honey, grated ginger, minced garlic, and sriracha sauce. Adjust the sriracha to your desired level of heat.

Mediterranean-inspired Sauce:
Ingredients:

- 1/4 cup Greek yogurt
- 1 tablespoon olive oil
- 1 tablespoon fresh lemon juice
- 1 teaspoon fresh dill, chopped
- 1 clove garlic, minced
- Salt and pepper to taste

Instructions:

In a bowl, combine Greek yogurt, olive oil, fresh lemon juice, chopped dill, minced garlic, salt, and pepper. Mix until smooth.

Sweet and Spicy Fusion Sauce:
Ingredients:

- 1/4 cup mayonnaise
- 2 tablespoons ketchup
- 1 tablespoon Sriracha sauce
- 1 tablespoon honey
- 1 teaspoon soy sauce
- 1/2 teaspoon garlic powder
- 1/2 teaspoon smoked paprika
- Salt and pepper to taste

Instructions:

In a bowl, whisk together mayonnaise, ketchup, Sriracha sauce, honey, soy sauce, garlic powder, smoked paprika, salt, and pepper. Adjust the ingredients to your taste.

These fusion burger creations and sauces offer a delightful blend of flavors from different cuisines. Whether you're craving the bold and spicy Tex-Mex fusion or want to explore global-inspired sauces, these recipes will take your burger experience to a whole new level.

Chapter 15: Healthier Burger Alternatives

If you're looking for healthier options without compromising on flavor, this chapter is for you. We'll explore two wholesome alternatives: Lettuce Wrapped Burgers and Sweet Potato Burger Buns.

Lettuce Wrapped Burgers

Ingredients:

- Large, sturdy lettuce leaves (iceberg or butter lettuce works well)
- Burger patties of your choice (beef, chicken, turkey, or veggie)
- Sliced tomatoes
- Sliced red onion
- Pickles
- Mustard, ketchup, or your preferred burger sauce
- Sliced cheese (optional)

Instructions:

Prepare the Burger Patties:

Season and cook your choice of burger patties to your preferred level of doneness.

Wash and Prepare Lettuce Leaves:

Carefully wash and pat dry the large lettuce leaves.

These lettuce leaves will serve as your burger bun alternative.

Assemble Your Lettuce Wrapped Burgers:

Lay out one large lettuce leaf as your "bottom bun."

Place the cooked burger patty on top.

Add sliced tomatoes, red onion, pickles, and your choice of cheese (if desired).

Top with another lettuce leaf as the "top bun."

Condiments and Sauce:

Add mustard, ketchup, or your preferred burger sauce to taste.

You can also add additional toppings like avocado, bacon, or sautéed mushrooms for extra flavor.

Serve and Enjoy:

Your Lettuce Wrapped Burger is ready to be enjoyed. It's a fresh and low-carb alternative to traditional burger buns.

Sweet Potato Burger Buns

Ingredients:

- 2 large sweet potatoes
- Olive oil
- Salt and pepper to taste
- Burger patties of your choice (beef, chicken, turkey, or veggie)
- Sliced tomatoes
- Sliced red onion
- Pickles
- Mustard, ketchup, or your preferred burger sauce
- Sliced cheese (optional)

Instructions:

Prepare the Sweet Potato Buns:

Preheat your oven to 375°F (190°C).

Wash and peel the sweet potatoes.

Slice the sweet potatoes into rounds, approximately 1/2 inch thick.

Place the sweet potato rounds on a baking sheet.

Drizzle with olive oil and season with salt and pepper.

Bake for about 20-25 minutes, flipping them halfway through, until they are tender and slightly crispy around the edges.

Prepare the Burger Patties:

Season and cook your choice of burger patties to your preferred level of doneness.

Assemble Your Sweet Potato Burger Buns:

Use two sweet potato rounds as your "bun."

Place the cooked burger patty on one sweet potato round.

Add sliced tomatoes, red onion, pickles, and your choice of cheese (if desired).

Top with another sweet potato round as the "top bun."

Condiments and Sauce:

Add mustard, ketchup, or your preferred burger sauce to taste.

Customize with additional toppings and condiments as desired.

Serve and Enjoy:

Your Sweet Potato Burger is a healthier, gluten-free alternative that adds a touch of natural sweetness to your burger experience.

These healthier burger alternatives provide creative ways to enjoy your favorite burger flavors while making nutritious choices. Whether you opt for lettuce-wrapped burgers for a low-carb option or sweet potato burger buns for a gluten-free twist, you'll savor every bite without sacrificing taste.

Chapter 16: Burger Breakfasts and Brunch

Burgers aren't just for lunch or dinner; they can make a fantastic breakfast or brunch option. In this chapter, we'll explore two delightful choices: the Breakfast Burger with Egg and the Brunch Burger with Hollandaise.

Breakfast Burger with Egg
Ingredients:
For the Burger Patties:

- 1 pound (450g) ground sausage or ground breakfast sausage
- Salt and pepper to taste

For the Toppings:

- Burger buns
- Fried or sunny-side-up eggs
- Sliced cheese (cheddar, Swiss, or your favorite)
- Cooked and crumbled bacon
- Sliced tomatoes
- Sliced red onion
- Sliced avocado (optional)
- Ketchup or hot sauce (optional)

Instructions:

Prepare the Burger Patties:

Shape the ground sausage into burger patties and season with salt and pepper.

Cook the Burger Patties:

Cook the sausage patties in your air fryer or on a stovetop griddle until they are cooked through and have a nice sear.

Assemble Your Breakfast Burger with Egg:

Place the cooked sausage patty on a burger bun.

Add a slice of cheese, allowing it to melt slightly from the heat of the patty.

Top with a fried or sunny-side-up egg, cooked to your preferred level of doneness.

Add cooked and crumbled bacon, sliced tomatoes, red onion, and avocado (if using).

Drizzle with ketchup or hot sauce if desired.

Serve and Enjoy:

Your Breakfast Burger with Egg is ready to be savored. It's a hearty and satisfying way to start your day.

Brunch Burger with Hollandaise
Ingredients:
For the Burger Patties:

- 1 pound (450g) ground beef or ground turkey
- Salt and pepper to taste
- Burger seasoning (optional)

For the Toppings:

- Burger buns
- Sliced ham or Canadian bacon
- Sliced cheese (Swiss or cheddar)
- Poached eggs
- Hollandaise sauce (store-bought or homemade)
- Fresh chives, chopped (for garnish)
- Sliced tomatoes (optional)
- Fresh spinach or arugula (optional)

Instructions:
Prepare the Burger Patties:
Season the ground beef or turkey with salt, pepper, and burger seasoning (if using).
Shape the seasoned meat into burger patties.
Cook the Burger Patties:
Cook the patties in your air fryer or on a stovetop griddle to your preferred level of doneness.
Assemble Your Brunch Burger with Hollandaise:
Place the cooked burger patty on a burger bun.
Add a slice of ham or Canadian bacon on top.
Lay a slice of cheese over the ham.
Top with a perfectly poached egg.
Drizzle hollandaise sauce generously over the entire creation.

Garnish with fresh chives.

For extra freshness, you can add sliced tomatoes and fresh spinach or arugula.

Serve and Enjoy:

Your Brunch Burger with Hollandaise is ready to be enjoyed. It's an indulgent and flavorful choice for a weekend brunch.

These burger breakfasts and brunch options bring a delicious twist to your morning or midday meal. Whether you prefer the hearty and savory Breakfast Burger with Egg or the indulgent Brunch Burger with Hollandaise, these recipes are perfect for those who love to enjoy burgers at any time of day.

Chapter 17: Burger Desserts and Sweets

Burgers can be sweet too! In this chapter, we'll explore two delectable choices: the Sweet Potato Burger Dessert and the Ice Cream Burger Sandwich.

Sweet Potato Burger Dessert

Ingredients:

- For the Sweet Potato "Bun":
- 2 large sweet potatoes
- Olive oil
- Cinnamon and sugar (optional)
- For the Filling:
- Vanilla ice cream
- Caramel sauce
- Chopped nuts (walnuts, pecans, or your choice)

Instructions:

1. Prepare the Sweet Potato "Buns":
2. Preheat your oven to 375°F (190°C).
3. Wash and peel the sweet potatoes.
4. Slice the sweet potatoes into rounds, approximately 1/2 inch thick.
5. Place the sweet potato rounds on a baking sheet.
6. Drizzle with olive oil and, if desired, sprinkle with a mixture of cinnamon and sugar.
7. Bake for about 20-25 minutes, flipping them halfway through, until they are tender and slightly caramelized.

Assemble the Sweet Potato Burger Dessert:

1. Once the sweet potato rounds are done, let them cool slightly.

2. Place a scoop of vanilla ice cream between two sweet potato rounds to create a "burger."
3. Drizzle with caramel sauce and sprinkle with chopped nuts.

Serve and Enjoy:

Your Sweet Potato Burger Dessert is ready to be enjoyed. It's a delightful and healthier alternative to traditional dessert burgers.

Ice Cream Burger Sandwich
Ingredients:

- Donut or cinnamon bun (store-bought or homemade)
- Ice cream (your favorite flavor)
- Chocolate sauce or hot fudge
- Sprinkles (optional)

Instructions:

1. Prepare the "Buns":
2. Use a glazed donut or cinnamon bun as your "bun."
3. Slice it in half horizontally.
4. Assemble the Ice Cream Burger Sandwich:
5. Place a generous scoop of your favorite ice cream on the bottom half of the bun.
6. Drizzle with chocolate sauce or hot fudge.
7. If you like, add a sprinkle of colorful sprinkles for extra fun.

Top and Serve:

1. Place the top half of the bun on the ice cream to complete the "burger."
2. Serve immediately.

Serve and Enjoy:

Your Ice Cream Burger Sandwich is ready to be savored. It's a sweet and indulgent treat for dessert lovers.

These burger desserts and sweet treats offer a playful twist on the traditional burger concept, adding a touch of sweetness to your culinary repertoire. Whether you prefer the wholesome Sweet Potato Burger Dessert or the delightful Ice Cream Burger Sandwich, these recipes are perfect for satisfying your sweet tooth.

Chapter 18: Burger Party Planning

Planning a burger-themed party is a fun and delicious way to gather friends and family for a memorable occasion. In this chapter, we'll explore two essential elements of hosting a successful burger party: Hosting a Burger Cookout and Setting up a Burger Toppings Bar.

Hosting a Burger Cookout

A burger cookout is a classic way to celebrate with friends and family. Whether you're cooking on a grill, stovetop griddle, or using an air fryer, here are some tips to make your burger cookout a hit:

Menu Planning:

- Choose a variety of burger types to accommodate different dietary preferences. Include classic beef burgers, chicken, turkey, and veggie options.

- Consider any dietary restrictions or allergies your guests may have and provide suitable alternatives.

- Prepare a selection of burger buns and alternatives like lettuce wraps and sweet potato rounds for low-carb and gluten-free options.

Burger Accompaniments:

- Offer a range of condiments and toppings such as lettuce, tomato, onion, pickles, cheese, bacon, sautéed mushrooms, and guacamole.

- Don't forget to include a selection of sauces like ketchup, mustard, mayonnaise, BBQ sauce, and various homemade burger sauces.

Sides and Snacks:

- Prepare a variety of sides like crispy air fryer fries, coleslaw, potato salad, and a selection of fresh salads.

- Offer snacks and appetizers like sliders, mini hot dogs, or vegetable platters with dips.

Beverages:

- Provide a variety of drinks, including water, soda, iced tea, and lemonade

- Consider offering a selection of craft beers, wine, or non-alcoholic options for adult guests.

Dessert:

- Keep the burger theme going with dessert-inspired burgers like the Sweet Potato Burger Dessert or Ice Cream Burger Sandwich from Chapter 17.

- You can also offer a range of sweet treats like brownies, cookies, or a dessert bar.

Burger Toppings Bar

Setting up a burger toppings bar allows guests to customize their burgers to their liking. Here's how to create a burger toppings bar:

Toppings and Condiments:

- Arrange a variety of toppings in separate bowls or containers. Include lettuce, tomato slices, onion rings, pickles, cheese slices, bacon, sautéed mushrooms, guacamole, and more.

- Provide an assortment of condiments, including ketchup, mustard, mayonnaise, BBQ sauce, hot sauce, and various homemade burger sauces.

Bun Options:

- Offer a selection of burger buns, including classic, whole wheat, and specialty buns like brioche or pretzel buns.
- Include lettuce leaves and sweet potato rounds for low-carb and gluten-free alternatives.

Tools and Utensils:

- Set out serving utensils, tongs, and plenty of napkins for guests to assemble their burgers easily.

- Provide small plates or trays for guests to carry their creations.

Beverage and Dessert Station:

- Set up a beverage station with a variety of drinks and an ice bucket.

- If you're serving dessert, create a separate dessert station with dessert-inspired burgers, sweet treats, and coffee or tea.

Decorations:

Decorate the toppings bar with burger-themed decorations like burger-themed banners, tablecloths, and fun signage.

Consider providing themed tableware like burger-themed plates and napkins.

With a well-planned burger cookout and a creatively designed burger toppings bar, your burger-themed party is sure to be a hit. Your guests will have a blast customizing their burgers and enjoying the delicious array of burger-inspired dishes and sides.

Chapter 19: Burger Leftovers and Repurposing

Don't let those leftover burgers go to waste! In this chapter, we'll explore two creative ways to reinvent and repurpose your burger leftovers: Reinventing Leftover Burgers and Burger-Stuffed Bell Peppers.

Reinventing Leftover Burgers

Ingredients:

- Leftover burger patties (beef, chicken, turkey, or veggie)
- Burger buns or other bread (if available)
- Additional toppings (lettuce, tomato, onion, pickles, cheese)
- Condiments (ketchup, mustard, mayonnaise, BBQ sauce)

Instructions:

Prepare the Leftover Burger Patties:

If you have leftover burger patties, gently reheat them in your air fryer or on a stovetop griddle until they're warmed through and have a slight crisp.

Revive the Bun (Optional):

If you have leftover burger buns or other bread, you can refresh them by lightly toasting them in the air fryer or oven.

Reconstruct the Burger:

Reassemble the burger using the leftover patty and any additional toppings you have on hand.

Add fresh lettuce, tomato, onion, pickles, cheese, or condiments to enhance the flavor.

Serve and Enjoy:

Your reinvented leftover burger is ready to be savored. It's a quick and delicious way to enjoy your burger leftovers in a fresh way.

Burger-Stuffed Bell Peppers
Ingredients:

- Leftover burger patties (beef, chicken, turkey, or veggie)
- Bell peppers (any color)
- Cooked rice (white, brown, or your choice)
- Tomato sauce or marinara sauce
- Shredded cheese (cheddar, mozzarella, or your favorite)
- Salt and pepper to taste

Instructions:
Prepare the Leftover Burger Patties:
If you have leftover burger patties, gently reheat them in your air fryer or on a stovetop griddle until they're warmed through and have a slight crisp.

Prep the Bell Peppers:
Cut the tops off the bell peppers and remove the seeds and membranes.

Prepare the Filling:
Crumble the leftover burger patties into a bowl.

Mix in cooked rice, tomato sauce or marinara sauce, shredded cheese, salt, and pepper. Combine until well-mixed.

Stuff the Bell Peppers:
Fill each bell pepper with the burger and rice mixture, pressing it down gently.

Bake or Air Fry:
Place the stuffed bell peppers in your air fryer or oven and cook until the peppers are tender and the filling is heated through and bubbly. This usually takes about 20-25 minutes at 350°F (175°C).

Serve and Enjoy:
Your Burger-Stuffed Bell Peppers are ready to be enjoyed. It's a creative way to turn your burger leftovers into a new and satisfying meal.

These creative recipes allow you to make the most of your burger leftovers by giving them a fresh and delicious twist. Whether you choose to reinvent your burgers with fresh toppings or transform them into Burger-Stuffed Bell Peppers, you'll be amazed at how versatile and flavorful your leftovers can be.

Chapter 20: Conclusion and Beyond

Final Thoughts on Air Fryer Burgers

Congratulations! You've reached the end of "Air Fryer Hamburgers," and I hope you've enjoyed this flavorful journey into the world of burger creations. Air fryers provide a convenient and efficient way to cook burgers, offering a crispy exterior and juicy interior that's hard to resist.

Throughout this cookbook, you've explored a wide range of burger recipes, from classic beef burgers to creative chicken, turkey, seafood, and veggie options. You've also delved into healthier alternatives, international flavors, and even dessert-inspired burgers. Plus, you've discovered tips for hosting burger parties, repurposing leftovers, and pairing your burgers with delightful beverages.

Remember, the versatility of air fryers allows you to experiment with various ingredients, seasonings, and toppings to create burgers that suit your taste preferences. Whether you're a burger purist or a culinary adventurer, there's a burger recipe in this cookbook for you.

As you continue your culinary journey, don't forget to explore the endless possibilities of your air fryer. It's not just for burgers; you can use it to prepare a wide array of dishes, from crispy appetizers to mouthwatering main courses and even delectable desserts.

Exploring More Air Fryer Recipes

If you're eager to expand your air fryer culinary repertoire beyond burgers, here are some ideas to get you started:

- Air Fryer Chicken Wings: Crispy on the outside, tender on the inside, and perfectly seasoned.
- Air Fryer Fries: Enjoy crispy fries with less oil and more flavor.
- Air Fryer Salmon: A quick and healthy way to prepare succulent salmon fillets.
- Air Fryer Vegetables: Roast a medley of vegetables with a touch of seasoning for a wholesome side dish.
- Air Fryer Desserts: Try making mini pies, churros, or even air-fried doughnuts for a sweet treat.
- Air Fryer Appetizers: Create crispy spring rolls, stuffed mushrooms, or mozzarella sticks for your next gathering.

The possibilities are endless with an air fryer, so don't hesitate to explore and experiment with your favorite ingredients and flavors.

Thank you for joining me on this burger-centric culinary adventure. I hope you continue to enjoy cooking and discovering new recipes with your air fryer. Whether you're preparing classic comfort food or trying something entirely new, the journey of cooking is filled with creativity, satisfaction, and delicious moments shared with loved ones.

Happy cooking and bon appétit!

www.ingramcontent.com/pod-product-compliance
Lightning Source LLC
Chambersburg PA
CBHW051258160726
47994CB00003B/1224